DON BROWN

UP & DOWN

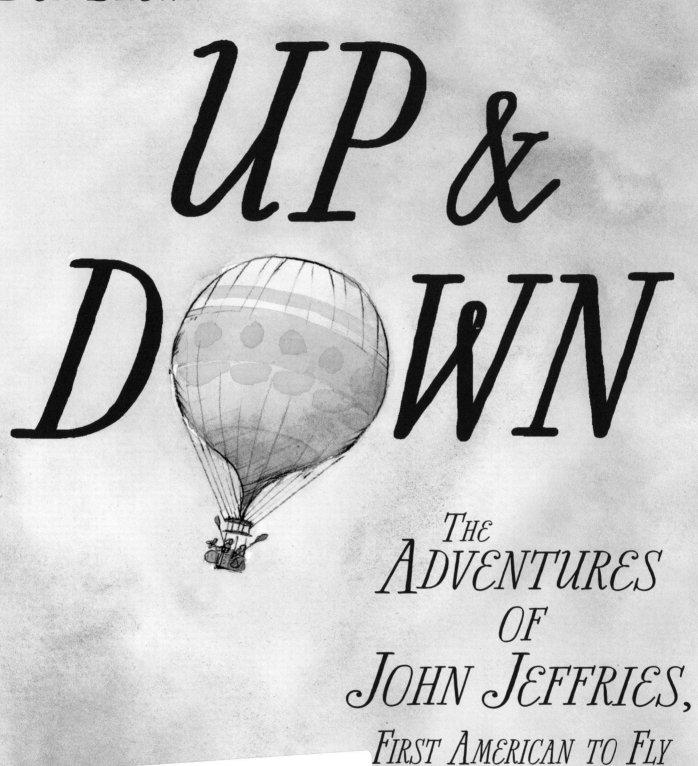

THE ADVENTURES OF JOHN JEFFRIES, FIRST AMERICAN TO FLY

Charlesbridge

When revolution came to America, poor Dr. John Jeffries of Boston made the unfortunate choice of remaining loyal to the king. At war's end, the king's rule was thrown out, and with it went Dr. Jeffries.

The doctor settled in London. There he cared for his
patients and kept a daily weather diary, for Jeffries was a man
devoted to useful science. It was this interest that would soon
send him soaring.

In France, the clever Montgolfier brothers were experimenting.
In 1782 they built a fire beneath a small bag, which filled with
hot air. To the brothers' delight, the bag rose to the ceiling.

A year later the brothers launched a bigger balloon and flew
their first passengers—a sheep, a rooster, and a duck—to the
amazement of the king and queen of France.

Then on November 21, 1783, two Frenchmen—a professor and a politician—boarded a Montgolfier balloon, floated upward, and became the first people to fly.

Rising above the streets of Paris, they tipped their hats to a crowd of spectators that included Benjamin Franklin. The balloon drifted for about twenty-five minutes and landed on the outskirts of the city.

Afterward, balloon mania exploded. Balloons decorated fans, skirts, clocks, and furniture. In London, one hundred fifty thousand people marveled at the first manned balloon flight in England.

Jeffries was swept up by the craze. But for him, it was all about weather. Having taken careful, daily weather notes on the ground for years, the thoughtful doctor wondered what discoveries he'd make in the clouds. "Nothing so much tends to enable us . . . to come at truth, as a variety of experiments," he said.

When French balloonist Jean-Pierre Blanchard visited London, Jeffries asked to accompany him on a voyage. The flight would allow him to measure temperature at different heights, observe the currents of air, and "throw some new light on the theory of winds in general."

Blanchard agreed. It wasn't the glories of science that won the Frenchman over, though. Jeffries promised to pay for his ride.

From a cramped yard in London, the two men—and a small dog brought by Jeffries—boarded an aerial car hanging beneath a linen balloon.

Blanchard filled his balloon with hydrogen gas instead of hot air, because hydrogen was lighter, giving the balloon greater lift. It also removed the need for a stove—and the risk of setting the balloon on fire.

At first the balloon staggered
upward, perching atop a stable for a
moment and knocking the funnels
off a chimney. Then it rose skyward.

9

Jeffries got to work. He measured temperature, humidity, and air pressure.

He corked bottles of air at different heights.

Blanchard rowed giant oars, trying to drive the balloon forward.

The two men ate cold chicken and drank wine.

After almost an hour and a half, the balloonists released some of the hydrogen and returned to earth. Jeffries was cold and tired. "I found myself . . . a little fatigued and feverish," he later said, "but a bowl of warm tea set me right."

Cheered by their success, the pair planned another, much more glorious flight: they would soar across the English Channel from Britain to France.

It had never been done. Success would bring fame and glory. But the price for failing could be drowning in the Channel.

Again at Jeffries's expense, they brought a balloon and equipment to the Dover cliffs overlooking the Channel. Rain and lashing wind kept them earthbound for a week. Then on January 7, 1785, the weather turned clear, frigid, and breezy. A bit of kite flying and the launch of two small balloons proved that the breeze blew toward France.

12

Jeffries and Blanchard filled the balloon with hydrogen gas from special casks. They attached two oars, a hand-cranked propeller, and a rudder to the aerial car.

Into the car went two cork life jackets, extra clothes, two small anchors and rope for landing, a compass, a barometer to measure how high they flew, and three ten-pound sacks of sand. The sand ensured that the balloon didn't leap too high in the sky.

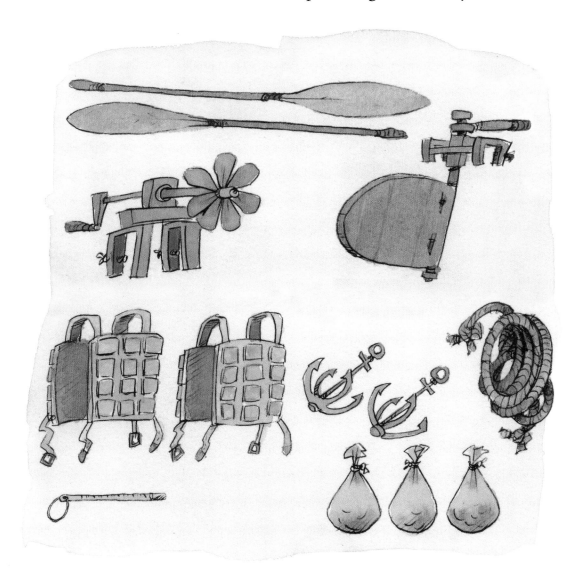

There would be no measuring the weather on this flight. "My chief object in this last aerial voyage," Jeffries said, "was the novelty and enterprise of being one of the first who passed across the sea from England." In other words, he was making the flight for the thrill of it.

Just before launch, Blanchard proved to be a rascal. Making a grab for fame and glory, he insisted the balloon was only strong enough to lift one man, and that man should be himself.

The sharp-eyed doctor spotted mischief: Blanchard wore an undercoat lined with heavy lead to weigh down the balloon. Jeffries told Blanchard to remove the coat. We can only guess at the men's moods as they finally boarded the balloon.

Then . . .

"Exactly at one o'clock . . . we rose slowly
and majestically from the cliff," said Jeffries.

Up and up Jeffries and Blanchard soared, spinning slowly as they went. Below them was an ever-changing, kaleidoscopic view of England, the Channel, and—far across the water—France.

As they climbed, the gas expanded in the higher, thinner atmosphere. The balloon fattened. Not wanting it to burst, the men released some of the gas.

Too much!

The balloon dropped. Out went one sack of sand. Then half of the second.

Lighter now, the balloon rose again and sailed toward France. All was quiet. They rode a breeze that would otherwise have whistled past their ears.

People shouting, horses neighing, wagons clattering, and the rest of life's jangly symphony were out of reach. They were wrapped in silence—a "kind of stillness . . . that could be felt," as Jeffries put it.

An hour into their voyage and halfway to
France, the balloon began sinking. The men cast
out the rest of the sand. The balloon rose, then
rapidly sank again. "We immediately threw out all
the little things we had with us, such as biscuits,
apples, . . . and after that one of our oars,"
said Jeffries.

Still they dropped.

21

The other oar was cast off. Then the rudder, propeller, anchors, and ropes.

Not enough.

"We began to strip ourselves, and cast away our clothing," recalled Jeffries.

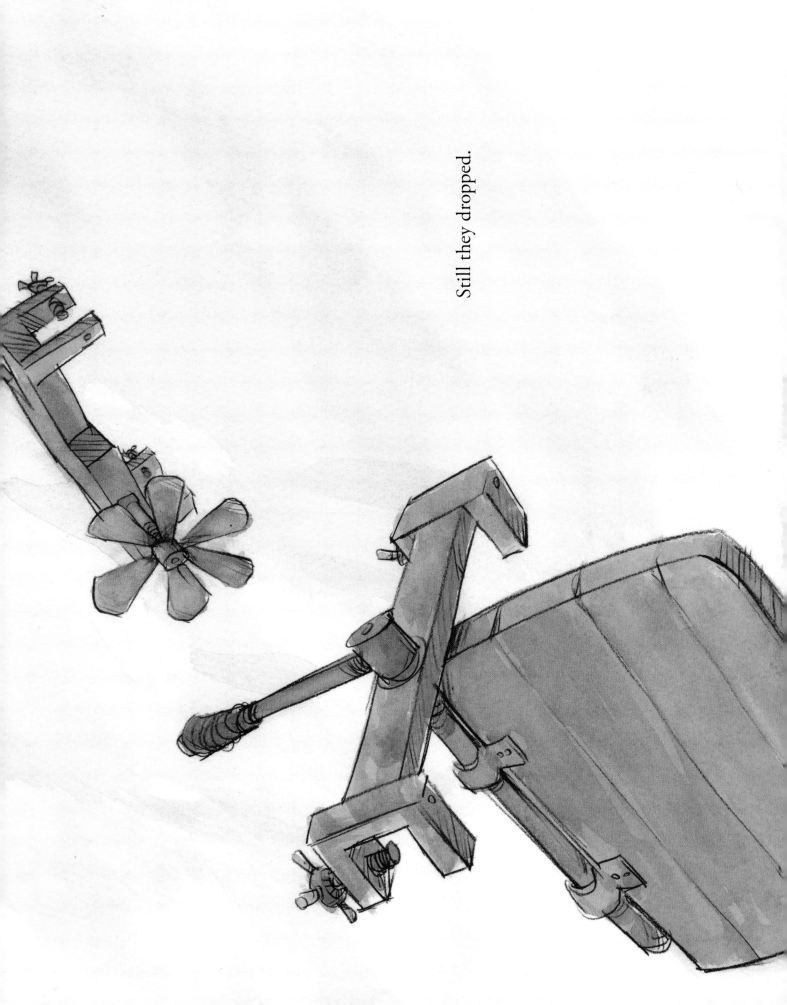

Still they dropped.

The men put on their cork life jackets and braced for a watery crash. But with the sea just yards away, they began to rise.

The rising and falling of the balloon puzzled Jeffries. Was the gas in the balloon somehow changing? Was it the atmosphere? The humidity in the air?

In the next moment, a more serious problem pressed him. "From the loss of our clothes, we were almost benumbed with cold," Jeffries said. Clad in their underwear, the men shivered in the frigid air as they rushed toward France.

Finally the coastline unfurled beneath them, then a beautiful patchwork of villages, fields, and roads.

They had crossed the Channel in exactly two hours.

But as Jeffries and Blanchard soared above a forest, the balloon began dropping again. Large, stabbing branches reached out to them.

"We cast away one cork jacket, and soon after it the other," said Jeffries.

The balloon still fell.

With nothing left to cast off, Jeffries proposed lightening themselves. Like two little boys with nowhere to go, the men relieved themselves.

It seemed to work!

As the balloon slowed its descent, Jeffries reached out and caught hold of the topmost branches of a tree. The balloon stopped and hovered in place.

With the balloon swaying uncertainly over their heads,
Jeffries and Blanchard pulled themselves to a clearing, where
they made a peaceful landing.

They had done it: glided across the Channel with the grace
of a seabird . . . and as nearly naked!

Onlookers rushed to their aid and gave them clothes to
wear, too.

Jeffries and Blanchard were cheered as heroes. The scientific societies of Paris made Jeffries an honorary member. Blanchard was richly rewarded by the king and went on to make the first balloon flight in America.

But Jeffries never flew again. By 1790 America had forgiven him for choosing the wrong side in the war. He returned to Boston and continued his work as a doctor—and as a lifetime weather watcher.

Today Dr. John Jeffries is still remembered, not for being the first American to fly, but for his devotion to useful science: National Weatherperson's Day is celebrated on his birthday.

More Hot Air: An Endnote

"Are you men or gods?"

Shocked villagers shouted the question at the passengers of a low-flying balloon.

They'd never seen one before—perhaps never even imagined one.

Elsewhere, a surprise landing by an unmanned balloon upset a group of peasants. Certain it was something evil, they tore it to pieces with pitchforks.

The eighteenth century was a world lit by fire, at the infancy of steam power, ignorant of evolution, and without a firm grasp of chemistry, biology, physics, or geology. The chance to look down at the ground was reserved for those willing to climb a tree or mountain. The idea of human flight was limited to legend and daydream. It's no wonder that balloon flight was greeted with astonishment and mania on a scale that is hard for us to imagine today. Hundreds of thousands of spectators crowded London and Paris to witness balloon launchings.

In this world we find Dr. John Jeffries and Jean-Pierre Blanchard.

They were an unlikely pair. Jeffries was a scientist with a healthy respect for data collection and a desire to expand the borders of knowledge. Blanchard was a shameless, self-serving daredevil. But let's not discount the "daredevil" label. Ballooning was risky. Early balloons sometimes tore open or burst into flames, sending their passengers plummeting to their doom.

Five months after Jeffries and Blanchard floated across the Channel, Jean-François Pilâtre de Rozier attempted to make the trip in reverse, but died in a crash. In 1819 Sophie Blanchard, the balloonist wife of Jean-Pierre, died in a fiery wreck.

Even today, a balloon crossing of the Channel holds inherent dangers. In 2012 two balloonists attempted to reenact the Jeffries and Blanchard flight. They, too, lifted off from Dover. As did their predecessors, they drifted in silence. Then the wind changed, keeping them over water and scudding parallel to the French coast. Using the balloon's radio, they learned about more favorable winds at a higher altitude. They were able to reach these winds given the craft's sophisticated equipment, but without the modern upgrades, the balloon might have ended up drifting over the expansive, unfriendly North Sea.

In 1793 Jean-Pierre Blanchard went on to make the first balloon flight in the Americas; George Washington watched as the balloon rose above Philadelphia. In 1808 the daring Frenchman had a heart attack and fell from his balloon. He died a year later from his injuries.

Dr. John Jeffries was the first person to conduct scientific research in the air. In 1790 he returned to Boston, where he became a popular and respected local doctor. He died in 1819, according to one report from "an inflammation in his bowels, originating in a hernia, occasioned by great exertions in his first aerial voyage."

BIBLIOGRAPHY

Bell, J. L. "Dr. John Jeffries: Physician, Loyalist, Aeronaut." Boston 1775 (blog). July 29–Aug. 5, 2006. http://boston1775.blogspot.com/2006/07/dr-john-jeffries-physician-loyalist.html.

Crouch, Tom. "Across the Channel by Balloon." *Air & Space Magazine*. Aug. 2013. http://www.airspacemag.com/history-of-flight/across-the-channel-by-balloon-11414318/?no-ist.

———. "In the Museum: Fashion Lighter Than Air." *Air & Space Magazine*. July 2009. http://www.airspacemag.com/history-of-flight/in-the-museum-fashion-lighter-than-air-137642301/.

———. *Lighter Than Air: An Illustrated History of Balloons and Airships*. Baltimore: Johns Hopkins University Press, 2009.

Elevado, Megan. "Balloon Mania." Cooper Hewitt Museum. June 4, 2013. http://www.cooperhewitt.org/2013/06/04/balloon-mania/.

Holmes, Richard. *The Age of Wonder: How the Romantic Generation Discovered the Beauty and Terror of Science*. New York: Pantheon Books, 2008.

———. *Falling Upwards: How We Took to the Air*. New York: Pantheon Books, 2013.

Hoskin, Dawn. "Flying High—230 Years Ago Today." Victoria and Albert Museum. Dec. 1, 2013. http://www.vam.ac.uk/blog/creating-new-europe-1600-1800-galleries/flying-high-230-years-ago-today.

Jeffries, Dr. John. *Two Aerial Voyages of Dr. Jeffries with Mons. Blanchard*. London: J. Robson, 1786. https://ia600907.us.archive.org/32/items/narrativeoftwoae00jeff/narrativeoftwoae00jeff.pdf.

Kim, Mi Gyung. "Balloon Mania: News in the Air." *Endeavour* 28 (Dec. 2004): 149–155. http://jhfc.duke.edu/triangleintellectualhistory/files/2014/07/IHS-mania04.pdf.

Kotar, S. L., and J. E. Gessler. *Ballooning: A History, 1782–1900*. Jefferson, NC: McFarland & Co., 2011.

May, Gustav. *Ballooning: A Concise Sketch of Its History and Principles*. London: Symons & Co., 1885. https://books.google.com/books?id=68oEAAAAMAAJ.

"Sketch of the Medical Life of the Late Dr. John Jeffries." *New-England Journal of Medicine and Surgery* 9 (Jan. 1820): 63–72. https://books.google.com/books?id=ldlNAQAAMAAJ.

Thatcher, James. *American Medical Biography*. Vol 1. Boston: Richardson & Lord and Cotton & Barnard, 1828. https://books.google.com/books?id=_PIUAAAAYAAJ.

University of Oxford. "The Surprising 'Balloon Mania' of Romantic Literature." Dec. 17, 2014. http://www.ox.ac.uk/news/2014-12-17-surprising-%E2%80%98balloon-mania-romantic-literature.

The URLs listed here were accurate at publication, but websites often change. If a URL doesn't work, you can use the internet to find more information.

Quotation Sources

Page 6: "Nothing so much . . . variety of experiments": Jeffries, p. 10.

Page 7: "throw some . . . winds in general": Jeffries, p. 11.

Page 11: "I found myself . . . set me right": Jeffries, p. 25.

Page 13: "My chief object . . . from England": Jeffries, p. 49.

Page 15: "Exactly at one . . . from the cliff": Jeffries, p. 42.

Page 20: "kind of stillness . . . that could be felt" [italics removed]: Jeffries, p. 52.

Page 21: "We immediately . . . our oars": Jeffries, p. 45.

Page 22: "We began . . . our clothing" [italics removed and spelling modernized]: Jeffries, p. 45.

Page 27: "From the loss . . . benumbed with cold" [spelling modernized]: Jeffries, p. 47.

Page 28: "We cast away . . . the other" [spelling modernized]: Jeffries, p. 47.

Page 36: "Are you men or gods?": Jean-Pierre Blanchard's account of his third aerial voyage, published in *Edinburgh Advertiser*, Sept. 24, 1784, and quoted in Kotar and Gessler, p. 28.

Page 37: "an inflammation . . . first aerial voyage" [spelling modernized]: "Sketch of the Medical Life of the Late Dr. John Jeffries," p. 70.

Author's Note

Many illustrations from the early balloon era show baskets in the shape of ships. I believe those illustrations were made not from observation but from the artists' imagination. It strikes me that experience would have taught the earliest balloonists that drifting in the wind makes the notion of a front or back of the basket meaningless. With that in mind, I drew the familiar, box-shaped basket.

Am I correct? Perhaps. Is there the chance I am wrong? Absolutely.

History is often clouded, as in the question of the balloon-basket shape. In those cases, I apply the facts as I understand them, and do my best to present an accurate story.

For the Hill family:
Kristi, Jim, Redmond,
Jeremy & Chris

At the time of publication, all URLs printed in this book were accurate and active.
Charlesbridge and the author are not responsible for the content or accessibility of any website.

Published by Charlesbridge
85 Main Street
Watertown, MA 02472
(617) 926-0329
www.charlesbridge.com

Library of Congress Cataloging-in-Publication Data
Names: Brown, Don, 1949– author.
Title: Up & down: the adventures of John Jeffries, first American to fly/written and
  illustrated by Don Brown.
Other titles: Up and down: the adventures of John Jeffries, first American to fly
Description: Watertown, MA: Charlesbridge, [2018] | Includes bibliographical references.
Identifiers: LCCN 2017012706 (print) | LCCN 2017051689 (ebook) | ISBN
  9781632896605 (ebook) | ISBN 9781632896612 (ebook pdf) | ISBN 9781580898126
  (reinforced for library use)
Subjects: LCSH: Jeffries, John, 1745–1819—Juvenile literature. | Balloonists—
  Massachusetts —Boston—History—Juvenile literature. | Ballooning—History—
  Juvenile literature. | Meteorology—Research—History—Juvenile literature. |
  Physicians—Massachusetts—Boston—History—Juvenile literature.
Classification: LCC TL620.J44 (ebook) | LCC TL620.J44 B76 2018 (print) |
  DDC 629.13092 [B]—dc23
LC record available at https://lccn.loc.gov/2017012706

Printed in China
(hc) 10 9 8 7 6 5 4 3 2 1

Illustrations done in Pitt oil-base pencil and watercolor on Saunders 90-pound hot-press
  watercolor paper
Display type set in Typnic Titling by Manuel Eduardo Corradine
Text type set in Garamond Pro by Adobe Systems Incorporated
Color separations by Colourscan Print Co Pte Ltd, Singapore
Printed by 1010 Printing International Limited in Huizhou, Guangdong, China
Production supervision by Brian G. Walker
Designed by Diane M. Earley